WEIGHTIER MATTERS
–THE RELATIONSHIP BETWEEN TITHES AND JUSTICE

WHEN I WAS A CHILD

Volume 1

DR. LANSTON M. SYLVESTER

authorHOUSE®

AuthorHouse™
1663 Liberty Drive
Bloomington, IN 47403
www.authorhouse.com
Phone: 833-262-8899

Published by AuthorHouse 03/21/2023

ISBN: 979-8-8230-0393-3 (sc)
ISBN: 979-8-8230-0392-6 (e)

Library of Congress Control Number: 2023904999

Print information available on the last page.

This book is printed on acid-free paper.

CONTENTS

DEDICATION

To: Marilyn Murphy

While others succumbed to their fears, you faced yours. The daunting decision to raise five children with G_d rather than 5 children in a degrading relationship. I thank you! I don't know how you did it! I don't know how a single woman who did not graduate from college, raised 5 children who have tasted the heights of academia and excelled in vocations. I don't know how you raised 5 children who are faithful to G_d and the church though they went to public schools. I don't know how you financially survived. I am in awe of you. I need no church to describe G_d to me; I need no pastor to tell me the characteristics of G_d, for I have seen it up close and personal.

This book is for you and all the women and men out there like you who give of themselves to the benefit of others. You gave and asked for nothing in return. You gave when you had nothing, while others took when they had everything. It is because of you that I can speak and write boldly.

I strive to make you proud and my failures are simply reminders that I can never repay you but I must never stop trying.

Ubuntu—I am because you are!

FOREWORD

In the beginning, G_d created the heavens and the earth. Among many things that this well-known biblical verse conveys, one of the most poignant is that G_d owns everything. He created it; thus, He owns it. A very simple concept.

Given G_d's ownership of everything, how are His created subjects (we humans) supposed to respond? For multiple millennia, the answer has been to love the Lord, "with all thy heart, and with all thy soul, and with all thy mind." What a reasonable declaration this is! G_d gave us the essence of who we are and expects us to recognize and honor Him with the essence of who we are.

As time progressed, we, as the stewards of the created order, were allowed to amass material possessions—food, clothing, houses, tools, transportation, art and artifacts, cattle and crops, flocks and fields, herds and harvests, and of course, money. What is the response to G_d based on these material possessions? For multiple decades, since the resurrection, the answer has been, "bring ye all the tithes into the storehouse." Given G_d's ownership of everything, what a reasonable declaration this is. Or is it?

The approach taken in this book seeks to answer the last question. This body of work, though not original in concept, is quite original in approach. In language that's void of seminary-laden terminology, ecclesiastical groupthink, and laity-laden parroting, the author describes the principled response to G_d's ownership of everything. The author refocuses our attention to the essence of our relationships with our Creator and not simply just the possessions from our Creator. In other words, to use a crude fictional analogy from childhood, is it better to have the goose or the golden egg?

The fact that you are considering reading this book suggests you are open to new information. Good for you! You'll be richly rewarded, not just because the information may be new, but that it is also well reasoned and true. If the previous suggestion is unfounded, and you are skeptical of this book and its contents, then you, too, will be richly rewarded. The author uses careful exegetical skill to arrive at an answer that does justice to G_d as Creator as well as to the responder as a steward of the possession and essence provided by our Creator.

Lastly, if you are fixed in your thinking and completely sold on the narrative that has been dispensed from pulpits for your entire life, then it's not likely you'd be reading this book. Your mind is fixed, and that's that. But if the temptation gets too irresistible and you do start reading, you will also be rewarded, though perhaps not as richly as the open-minded or skeptic. Your reward will be that the author affirms the need for us to respond with our possessions to our Creator's beneficence. The efficacy of this response is grounded in the essence of who we are, what G_d has done (and continues to do), and what kind of relationship we seek to have with G_d. Make no mistake, you will be challenged—not to upset you, deride you, or chastise you but to make you think!

I could go on to tell you about the professional credentials of Dr. Lanston M. Sylvester, his academic acumen, his penchant for pastoral provocation toward piety, his love for G_d and His church, his childhood exploits with mischief (we grew up together as teenagers in Brooklyn), and his maturation to the man that he is now and is yet to be by G_d's grace. I could tell you about his principled stand on what the Word of G_d has declared as true regardless of what the culture or the conference may say. I could tell you all of that and more so you can better understand the man, the Christ follower who was driven to write this body of work. But it's better if you get that firsthand by reading and absorbing the contents of this book. Enjoy!

Lyndon Davis

PREFACE

When I was a child, I spoke as a child, I understood as
a child, I thought as a child; but when I became a man,
I put away childish things. For now, we see in a mirror,
dimly, but then face to face. Now I know in part, but
then I shall know just as also I am known.
                                    —1 Corinthians 13:11, 12 NKJV

There is no room in Christianity for divergent views. If you have a
divergent view, you may be labeled a heretic. From the onset of the
Roman Empire making Christianity legal, there has also been the
establishment of what is considered orthodox teaching. Orthodox
teaching according to the Holy Roman Empire was comprised of the
Trinity, doctrine of the church or ecclesiology, the authority of the
pope or apostolic succession, and the sacraments. If you broke away
from these "orthodox teachings" and became part of the Protestant
faith, Sola Scriptura became your foundation, with most of the
scriptural interpretations lending themselves to Roman Catholic
teachings. In times past, if you were labeled a heretic—someone
who believes differently than orthodoxy—there was the possibility of
losing one's life or being excommunicated. Today, members may be
disfellowshipped or simply leave a church in hope of finding others
with similar views.

The *When I Was a Child* series will address and take a new look at
traditional biblical teachings and how they have been interpreted and
understood. The name of the overall series was adopted to mark the

difference between how a child thinks and how an adult should think. One of the most impactful quotes is from the book, *Education*:

Every human being, created in the image of God, is endowed with a power akin to that of the Creator—individuality, power to think and to do. The men and women in whom this power is developed are those who bear responsibilities, who are leaders in enterprise, and who influence character. It is the work of True Education to develop this power, to train young people to be thinkers, and not mere reflectors of other people's thought. Let students be directed to the source of truth, to the vast fields opened for research in nature and revelation. Let them contemplate the great facts of duty and destiny, and the mind will expand and strengthen.

Instead of producing educated weaklings, institutions of learning may send forth men and women who are strong to think and act—individuals who are masters and not slaves of circumstances, individuals who possess breadth of mind, clearness of thought, and the courage of their convictions.

I realize that religion by nature seeks to control. This reality comes in direct conflict with those who do not seek to be reflectors of other people's thoughts. Unfortunately, established denominations only seek to make others believe what they believe. "When an organization loses sight of its mission, then its mission becomes self-preservation" (Alvin Kibble). Thus, this is not an indictment of one religious group but rather all groups unless it has put in place the room for discussion on beliefs.

Religion and denominations, even nondenominations, engage in making people believe what they believe rather than giving people the tools to search the scriptures. This book attempts to begin the process of challenging believers to go back to the Bible and look anew at the Word of G_d. People often quote others to uphold their beliefs on a particular matter, but the Bible gives insight to the methodology that should be incorporated when hearing or reading something new:

> Then the brethren immediately sent Paul and Silas away by night to Berea. When they arrived, they went into the synagogue of the Jews. These men were more fair-minded than those in Thessalonica, in that they received the word with all readiness, and searched the Scriptures daily to find out whether these things were so. Therefore, many of them believed, and also not a few of the Greeks, prominent women as well as men. (Acts 17:10, 11 NKJV)

The reality of this text reveals that one must go through a process to receive the scriptures to consider something that they had never heard before. Paul and Silas went to Berea and into the place of worship of the Jews. The synagogue was not only the place of worship but also the place of learning. Three things needed to receive the Word that G_d has for you may be learned from the Bereans:

1. And the worshippers who were there were more fair-minded. The word for fair-minded means "noble" or of noble birth. The Bereans conducted themselves in a noble way. Hearing something that you disagree with should not cause you to act in an ignoble manner.
2. They received the Word with all readiness. They did not have a divided heart. They did not listen to Paul and Silas while they were trying to rush home to watch their favorite movie. They gave the message that Paul and Silas were giving their full attention. How many times do many come to the house of G_d with divided hearts? They cannot give the message their full attention because their minds are on their plans; they have their minds on their problems; or they have their minds on their pain. Today, G_d says to ready your mind on His promises.

3. The Bereans searched the scriptures daily. They did not search the Word only when they had problems. They searched the Word so they may know the will, the work, and the way of G_d. They did not read the scriptures daily; they searched the scriptures daily. The difference between reading the scriptures and searching the scriptures is that one method stays on the surface, while the other method mines the Word of G_d. One method does not require looking for anything. The other method has intent and purpose.

This book, and the remainder of the series, will undoubtedly challenge believers. It will pose questions. Questions are used by both G_d and Satan. Satan asks questions that creates doubt in the Word of G_d. He questioned Eve, "did G_d say?" It was a question that led to doubting the plain Word. However, questions from G_d cause self-examination, reflection, and one's condition. I hope you will receive this book as the latter.

INTRODUCTION

For the love of money is a root of all kinds of evil, for which some have strayed from the faith in their greediness and pierced themselves through with many sorrows.

—1 Timothy 6:10 NKJV

"Some people got to have it; some people really need. Listen to me, why all do things, do things bad things with it" are the lyrics to "For the Love of Money." The aforementioned scripture by the apostle Paul is known by many, but the message falls short of entering the heart. In the culture of wealth that has developed in the church, in which the blessings of G_d are evaluated and understood by monetary value, many have strayed from the faith.

There is a need for understanding the Bible. Seventh-day Adventists keep the Sabbath, but Baptists and Pentecostals and other denominations believe that when Jesus died, He fulfilled the obligation to keep Saturday as the Sabbath. They also believe that was for the Jews, and the Jews were not under grace but under law.

Seventh-day Adventists practice returning a tithe and giving an offering. They believe that is still required following the Old Testament teaching. Why? Isn't that under the Jews' requirement? Why do Baptists and Pentecostals return a tithe but do not keep the Sabbath?

Seventh-day Adventists do not believe in the practice of circumcision as required for salvation; nor do Baptists or Pentecostals. Wow, finally an agreement! This book seeks to help simplify, if not clarify, the issue of the tithe, but finding balance is a difficult thing.

On one side we have the prosperity gospel and its various forms misleading millions. And on the other, you have many who equate holiness with poverty. Both are wrong, and both are exacerbated by ungodly individuals who lead many to their perils. Money is important; money is necessary; money is a defense. But money is not G_d. Yet many have abandoned true faith to worship at the altar of greed. There are ministers who use the Word of G_d to have poor people purchase private jets and pastors who pilfer the people and fleece the flock of G_d for personal gain.

This book does not seek to address these ills that permeate the church of the living G_d. This book will not address individual failings in following mammon. Instead, this book looks at a system, established by religion, that causes people to believe a lie. This system seeks to control not only their faith and understanding of G_d but also their finances and their understanding of money. To be clear, the Bible never intended for the people's money to take care of a religion over and above their families. The Bible never intended for people to be burdened to bring money every week to pay for a clergy that does not meet their needs. The Bible was never intended to promote a teaching of stewardship in which people take care of pastors rather than their mothers, fathers, grandmothers, and grandfathers. I have seen this evil.

It is dangerous to believe in something that is not true or is no longer applicable. Is it possible for something to be a command from G_d, a practice of the people of G_d, and yet it was not meant to last forever? Are there things in the Bible that pointed to Christ and were supposed to be practiced for a time? And were there principles and practices in scripture that showed what it meant to be "in Christ"? Is there a difference? Is there a difference between the Old and New Covenants? If so, what is it? This is at the heart of many divisions among religions and Christian denominations.

This book offers a glimpse for believers to take a fresh look at what they give, how they give, why they give, and to whom they give. The tithe has the same position as circumcision. The practice of circumcision and the practice of tithes had a greater meaning and purpose than taking off the foreskin on the male genitalia and more than giving 10 percent of your income. The church has moved on from mandating the removal of the foreskin because it has come to an understanding of its greater meaning. Yet the church remains satisfied with 10 percent tithing without approaching its greater meaning. Let's begin our journey.

CHAPTER 1

The Origin of the Tithe

Then Melchizedek king of Salem brought out bread and
wine; he was priest of God Most High. And he blessed
him and said: "Blessed be Abram of God Most High,
Possessor of heaven and earth; and blessed be God Most
High, who has delivered your enemies into your hand."
And he gave him a tithe of all.

—Genesis 14:18–20 NKJV

Rent, medical bills, prescription drugs, food, clothing. Many churches
teach that 10 percent of your income is required by G_d and comes
before taking care of these necessities. If you fail to give G_d His first,
it reveals a lack of faith. It is called a tithe. Is this really true? Why does
G_d need my money? Where in the Bible is this tithe required? When
did this tithe teaching begin? Does it still apply today for believers?

When G_d created the male Adam and the female Adam (Genesis 5:2),
He gave instructions regarding food, sex, work, rest, and dominion.
He placed restrictions on how man should eat, work, rest, and have
dominion. Man was not meant to simply be a consumer; he must also
give. After sin, man's struggle to give has been evident. Man wants,
man desires, and man seeks to have no restrictions or oversight. He has
abandoned the aspect of rest. He has lost the concept of righteous work,
and he desires dominion over his fellow man.

In many ways, the Old Testament is G_d dealing with man's inability to live out the plan of G_d and His pursuit to save man from himself. The Old Testament chronicles this pursuit of G_d from Adam to Noah. After the flood, G_d repopulated the earth through Noah's sons and their wives. Noah's three sons—Shem, Ham, and Japheth—and their descendants will make up the remaining story of the Old Testament, with Shem's line being preeminent.

The line of Shem produced Eber, who is the father of the Hebrews and the origin of the word "Hebrew." Ultimately, from the line of Shem, we are introduced to Abram, who G_d would call and be renamed Abraham. It is here that we are first introduced to the concept of tithing.

Sometimes you can avoid a fight; sometimes you can't. To keep peace with Lot, his brother's son, Abram gave Lot and his herdsmen the choice of land, and Abram willingly took the remaining land to keep peace with a family member. This, by itself, gives insight into the spirit of the man named Abram. However, a person's meekness should never be taken as a sign of weakness.

Lot chose the best land. But many times in life, what seems to be the best brings the most trouble. Lot settled on what was considered prime property; it was the most fertile land of the area. It would later serve as the outskirts of Sodom and Gomorrah, known for its opulence and luxury. Ezekiel declared that the sins of Sodom and Gomorrah were not simply of a sexual nature. The sins of Sodom and Gomorrah were more complex, less visible to the naked eye.

> As I live, says the Lord God, "neither your sister Sodom nor her Daughters have done as you and your daughters have done. Look This was the iniquity of your sister Sodom: She and her daughter had pride, fullness of food, and abundance of idleness; neither did she strengthen the hand of the poor and needy. And they were haughty and committed abomination before me; therefore, I took them away as I saw fit. (Ezekiel 16:48–50 NKJV)

The area was a land that facilitated wealth and comfort. However, there was an inherent danger because many desired the land and the wealth attached to it. Kings desired the land, and a war broke out between four kings—Amraphel, king of Shinar; Arioch, king of Ellasar; Chedorlaomer, king of Elam; and Tidal, king of nations—against five kings: Bera, king of Sodom; Birsha, king of Gomorrah; Shinab, king of Admah; Shemeber, king of Zeboiim; and Zoar, the king of Bela. As a result, Lot and his family were taken as prisoners of war. They seemed to be out of luck and out of hope. All that Lot had envisioned became a nightmare. The wealth he hoped to acquire, the comfort he desired to give his family, and the success he dreamed of having became a nightmare as he watched his family and servants become the property of the victorious kings.

Abram learned of his nephew's predicament, and the man of peace became a man of war. The man who was quick to defer to his nephew and who, by every right, could have left his nephew to his own demise rose to the occasion to save his brother's son. Blood is thicker than water. Blood is more valuable than gold or silver. Abram organized 318 of his trained servants, born in his own house, to pursuit the armies that took his nephew captive. The Lord granted Abram victory and showed mercy to Lot and his family. That should be the end of the story. But the Bible was written to reveal Christ. The Old Testament uses the lives of people to extract aspects of what the Messiah would accomplish. The Old Testament also uses objects to give insight into the work of the Messiah.

On obtaining victory over his nephew's captors and while collecting the spoils of war, Abram is confronted by the priest and ling of Salem, Melchizedek. He approached Abram and served him bread and wine. As he served Abram the bread and wine, Melchizedek proceeded to bless Abram. It was because he served Abram that Abram's response was to give him a tithe of the spoils. Why was this encounter between Melchizedek and Abram significant? What does this encounter have to do with believers in the twenty-first century?

3

This encounter is the foundation of the establishment of believers giving one-tenth of their increase. The encounter takes on symbolism as the type-antitype format is used to interpret the encounter. Melchizedek represents Christ; Abram—not Abraham—represents those who would believe. The bread and wine represent the body and blood of Christ that would be sacrificed and willingly offered. But what does the tithe represent? What did Abram's response of giving one-tenth of the spoils of war mean?

Lessons

- Tithe is introduced in the context of a broken relationship.
- Tithe is given after victory over an enemy.
- Tithe is given after the recovery of the captured.
- Tithe is given to someone greater who served someone lesser.
- Tithe is given from increase.

CHAPTER 2

The Meaning of the Tithe

> Now consider how great this man was, to whom even the patriarch Abraham gave a tenth of the spoils. And indeed, those who are the sons of Levi, who receive the priesthood, have a commandment to receive tithes from the people according to the law, that is, from their brethren, though they have come from the loins of Abraham.
>
> —Hebrews 7:4–7 (NKJV)

Type-Antitype

One of the primary purposes of the Old Testament is to establish how G_d would save humanity through the Messiah, who would come to die and pay the price (redeem) for humanity's freedom from the penalty of sin. It is a debt that could not be paid by sinful humans; it would have to be paid by the innocent. The Old Testament used the lives of many men and women to highlight characteristics that the Messiah would have and prophecies the Messiah would fulfill. These aspects are called "types"; the Messiah Himself would be the "antitype," or the reality.

Some examples of types of Christs are Joseph, Moses, David, Esther, and Abigail. Aspects of a person's life were highlighted in scripture to point to the reality of what and how the Messiah would accomplish salvation on behalf of the universe. Melchizedek also fulfills this paradigm as a type of Messiah or Christ. The book of Hebrews highlights Melchizedek to show what Christ has accomplished. Thus, in this pericope of scripture in Genesis 14, the encounter of Abram to Melchizedek is critical to the believer in Christ for what he has accomplished as he has fulfilled the aspect of the life of Melchizedek.

Certain characteristics immediately jump out at us. For example, Melchizedek is without history. It is not known who his father and mother were. He was both a priest and a king. These are the aspects of his life:

> So also, Christ did not glorify Himself to become High Priest, but it was He who said to him: "You are my son, today I have begotten you." As He also says in another place: you are a priest forever after the order of Melchizedek. (Hebrews 5:5, 6 NKJV)

The characteristics of Melchizedek's and its correlation to the Christ do not end with priest and king or his history. Melchizedek comes to Abram and offers him bread and wine. For Christians reading this book, you understand that bread and wine are symbols used to represent the body and blood of Christ, respectively. Thus, on Abram's victory over the kings who had taken his nephew as a prisoner of war, Melchizedek serves Abram bread and wine and proceeds to bless him. The order is important. The bread and wine were served, and the blessing was given before the tithe was given as a response. The basis of giving a tithe is not to receive a blessing but because a blessing was already given.

As a response to the blessing of Melchizedek, Abram offers a tenth, or a tithe, of the spoils he secured from those he defeated. Why one tenth? Why one tenth of the spoils from the victory and not from the wealth he attained throughout his financial life? The number ten is significant in scripture as it pertains to the law of G_d. The scriptures also state that if you break one, you are guilty of all. Thus, in giving Melchizedek one tenth, Abram was declaring faith in the coming Messiah, who would give His body and blood for salvation. And as an act of faith in this reality, Abram would give a deposit of his righteousness that could only be fulfilled in the sacrifice that would come as promised. Abram's righteousness would be dependent on Christ's sacrifice. Abram and the Jews would never be saved by keeping the law or by their own righteousness but only through the merits of the One who would come and offer His bread and wine. At its core, the tithe symbolizes righteousness by faith.

Another important detail that we must acknowledge is that Abram returned tithe, not Abraham. Melchizedek appeared to Abram before G_d changed his name. Melchizedek appeared to Abram before G_d promised him an heir. The "ha" added to Abram's name only took place after Ishmael was born and after he heeded the counsel of Sarai to sleep with Hagar. G_d presented the promised sacrifice before he promised anything else to Abram. Abram recognized his own unrighteousness and accepted the bread and wine. And in return, believed that his righteousness and obedience to the law would rest in the merits of the One who would make the sacrifice. This reality would once again be played out in the life of Abraham in Genesis 22. Obedience to the law was preceded by faith in the promise.

Some may question this reality of law and faith in the life of Abraham. There are those who believe that the law came under Moses. This is incorrect. The law was codified under Moses for the purpose of defining a nation totally under G_d. According to Genesis 26:5, "because Abraham obeyed My voice and kept My charge, My commandments, My statutes, and My laws." The commands of G_d have always existed in the hearts of man, written in nature, spoken by the prophets, and manifest in the Son of G_d. Abraham was faithful and obedient before there was the appearance of a Jew. He was the father of the Jews, who were ethnically and nationally Babylonian, modern-day Iraq.

Let us, therefore, have clarity on the meaning of the tithe. The tithe is not simply one tenth of someone's income. The original meaning of the tithe was a response of faith based on a promise that was made. Christ would sacrifice His body (bread) and blood (wine), and in return, those who accept that sacrifice would take on His righteousness. As Melchizedek's bread and wine symbolized the body and blood of Christ, so Abram's tithe would symbolize man's righteousness in Christ.

The scriptures do not teach and have never taught that the Jews or believers in G_d before the cross were saved by the law. Jesus is the Lamb of G_d, slain from the foundation of the world. This means that the plan to save man through the merits and sacrifice of Christ were instituted before a Jew ever walked on the earth. Let that sink in! Unfortunately, the children of Abraham perverted the teachings of G_d much in the same way Christianity has done in our days.

Righteousness is the outgrowth of and response to the sacrifice offered for salvation. The act of these two individuals, Abram and Melchizedek, is forever etched as an example of the relationship and cooperation between God and man in the salvation process. To give a tenth is not paying G_d. To return a tithe was never meant as a reciprocal basis for receiving a blessing. The experience between Melchizedek and Abram forever established that the tithe, at its core, pointed to the sacrifice that would be offered and fulfilled in Christ and man's adequate response to that sacrifice. Therefore, since the tithe pointed to the work of Christ, that work was fulfilled at the cross.

If the bread and wine were symbols and the giving of the tithe was a symbol or shadow that pointed to the real, why are we still returning tithe when the real has appeared? If the true bread and wine have been offered, why would the people of G_d still offer a symbol of righteousness and not true righteousness itself?

Symbols

In Galatians 4, the apostle Paul writes that Abraham's two wives represented the freewoman and the bondwoman. He then wrote that these women are symbols. Hagar is Mount Sinai, but Sarah represents the Jerusalem that is above. The book of Hebrews continues with the symbolic teaching regarding Melchizedek and Christ. So consider the following:

Type	Antitype
Melchizedek	Christ
Bread and Wine	Body and blood
Abraham	Faithful believers
Tithe	Righteousness/justice

The tithe represents a symbol of righteousness and justice just as the bread and wine represent the actual body and blood of Christ. Christ did not give of Himself so we could give Him money. He did not sacrifice His life so His people could give Him money. He gave of Himself so we could become the righteous through Him.

> For if Abraham was justified by works, he has something to boast about, but not before G_d. For what does the Scripture say? "Abraham believed G_d, and it was accounted to Him for righteousness." (Romans 4:2–3 NKJV)

Since the tithe represents righteousness, it is imperative to understand that the tithe was originally based on a relationship. The tithe is not simply a symbol of righteousness as it relates to religion. It is a symbol of righteousness based on relationships. Relationships are the arena where sin was manifested, and relationships would be the arena where man's righteousness would be the evidence to a fallen world. This will ultimately be validated by the usage of the tithe in Israel.

Income or Increase

Another aspect of tithes that is discussed among members of churches is whether one should pay on the gross or the net of their incomes? And while we will not spend time on the aspect of gross or net, we will look at the aspect of income or increase. Is income the same as increase? Is there any evidence that the two are synonymous, or is this just a perspective taken as a fact? Many point to Proverbs 3:9 to uphold this belief:

> Honor the Lord with your possessions, And with the first fruits of all your increase. (Proverbs 3:9 NKJV)

There are several things to examine here. First and foremost, income is not increase. In most churches today, income is taught as increase, but this is not accurate. Income, "refers to the amount of money, property, and other transfers of value received over a set period of time in exchange for services or products." In other words, income is based on the barter principle. In the United States and most of the Western world, individuals are paid based on their expertise and time offered to a company in exchange for a monetary value. A transfer of goods, services, and time takes place. Income is based on the ability and works of man. In the Bible, this is not what increase means.

Increase is not a barter. Increase is not based on the works, abilities, or accomplishments of individuals. Increase is strictly based on the providence and provision of G_d. Increase is never used in connection with the labor man is to engage in. Increase is not based on the planting and watering of man.

Israel was primarily an agrarian society. And the scriptures use this economy to teach spiritual lessons of former rain and latter rain. And yes, increase.

> Then the earth shall yield her increase; G_d, our own G_d, shall bless us. (Psalm 67:6 NKJV)

> Yes, the Lord will give what is good; And our land will yield its increase. (Psalm 85:12 NKJV)

> You shall truly tithe all the increase of your grain that the field produces year by year. (Deuteronomy 14:22 NKJV)

And in the fifth year you may eat its fruit, that it may yield to you its increase: I am the Lord your G_d. (Leviticus 19:25 NKJV)

Israel was holiness to the Lord, The first fruits of His increase. All that devour him will offend; Disaster will come upon them, says the Lord. (Jeremiah 2:3 NKJV)

Now may he who supplies seed to the sower, and bread for food, supply and multiply the seed you have sown and increase the fruits of your righteousness. (2 Corinthians 9:10 NKJV)

With certainty, when you experience increase in your life, it is because of G_d. That is increase. You didn't earn it. You didn't work for it. When Abram gave Melchizedek the tithe, it was not from his income. He did not give a tithe of what his hands labored for. Abram gave Melchizedek a tithe from the spoils of war because G_d had increased him and given him victory over his enemies.

Now some may see a discrepancy in this view. Some Bible translations read that Abram gave a tithe of all that he had. He tithed everything. But is everything, everything? Context in the Bible is of extreme importance. Thus, the context of Abram giving Melchizedek a tithe of "everything" is clarified in Genesis 14:16: "He recovered all the goods and brought back his relative Lot and his possessions, together with the women and other people." All the goods is the everything.

Firstfruits

Another misinterpretation of scripture is the understanding of firstfruits. Some connect firstfruits with tithes. They are neither the same things nor connected. Firstfruit has nothing to do with the gross or net of your income. Firstfruits is an agricultural term that was used in Israel to further teach spiritual lessons. Firstfruits was the first agricultural produce of a particular season that was given to G_d as an offering.

Since it was the first agricultural produce of a particular season, more than one firstfruit could be given in a year.

It is dangerous to remove the biblical applications of terms and concepts to force them to fit into our context for the purpose of encouraging—yes, manipulating—people to give more. When we replace increase with income and firstfruits with gross income, we no longer can move into the spiritual application. We lose the meaning of Christ being the firstfruit of those who have died.

Lessons

- A tithe is a symbol of righteousness and justice.
- The foundation of returning tithes is the giving of the sacrifice of the One who is greater.
- A tithe is based on the increase of G_d, not the work of man.
- A tithe is a representation of righteousness by faith.

CHAPTER 3

Different Use of Tithes in Israel

At the end of every third year you shall bring out the tithe of your produce of that year and store it up within your gates. And the Levite, because he has no portion nor inheritance with you, and the stranger and the fatherless and the widow who are within your gates, may come and eat and be satisfied, that the Lord your G_d may bless you in all the work of your hand which you do.

—Deuteronomy 14:28, 29 NKJV

Israel had become a nation. During their wilderness experience, the Levites were chosen and separated to be servants of the tabernacle (Numbers 8). They would receive no inheritance when they entered the Promised Land. They were to be sustained by the people's faithfulness to the service of G_d. The priest would serve the people in the place of G_d and in return, be sustained by the righteousness (right doing) of the people. The original meaning of the tithe is reinforced throughout the Israelite economy.

The tithe was also based on Israel's agricultural economy. Therefore, the tithe most often took the form of animals, fruit, vegetables, and grains. It was only when Israel had to travel great distances that the tithe might be exchanged for its monetary value. Deuteronomy 14, possibly more than any other chapter, outlines and deals with how the tithe was applied and functioned in the Israelite economy.

The Israelites were reminded that they are G_d's holy people. Being His holy people is manifest by what they eat and the harvest they gather. It is interesting that holiness is associated with how man (Israelites) related to and treated nature. This is a recall to man's purpose in having dominion over what G_d has given humankind. What is man's response to the goodness of G_d and His provisions?

The Israelites were to return a tithe on grain, wine, oil, and their flocks, so that in everything they did and in everything they were engaged, they would learn the fear of the Lord. Again, as it was in the beginning of Abram's giving a tithe to Melchizedek, the tithe would be a response to the grace of G_d. The goodness of G_d through nature would be recognized by His people. But this is just the beginning. The greatest aspect of G_d's creation is man.

The tithe also highlighted the fundamental aspect of holiness: relationships. Every third year the Israelite economy was to dedicate the tithe to four groups: the Levite (because he had no inheritance), the stranger (because he had no country), the fatherless (because he had no father, no root), and the widow (because he had no spouse, no support). While the tithe took care of the priests and Levites every year, the three other groups were not to be forgotten. Righteousness and holiness cannot be extricated from relationships. Tithing was to be a constant reminder of how the least of these were to be not only remembered but how they were to be treated and looked after.

Churches that receive tithes from people but neglect to use the collected monies to lift the least, lost, or left behind while claiming to collect holy money do a disservice to the principles of G_d. Tithing in the Old Testament did not only go to the priests or Levites but to uplifting humanity. This is the essence and manifestation of holiness. Putting money in a collection plate or a tithe envelope and think that the responsibility has been fulfilled is foolish. Churches now engage in separatism. Churches, especially in white evangelicalism, uphold principles of racism that are antithetical to the teachings of scripture or the use of tithe.

An article from a magazine of a prominent denomination proposed that it is a given that the tithe is used for the promotion of the gospel. While this sounds good, there is no scriptural support for that position. If taking care of the priest and the Levites is promoting the gospel, then I concede. The problem exists in the transference of application from the Old Testament to the New Testament. The sanctuary is believed to have been replaced by the church building. The priests have been replaced by the pastors, and therefore, tithing goes to the pastors (priests) and teachers (Levites). This is the fundamental belief of many in the church. However, no such transference is applicable.

For this Melchizedek, King of Salem, priest of the Most High G_d, who met Abraham returning from the slaughter of the kings and blessed him, to whom also Abraham gave a tenth part of all, first being translated king of righteousness, and then also king of Salem, meaning king of peace, without father, without mother, without genealogy, having neither beginning of days nor end of life, but made like the Son of G_d, remains a priest continually. Now consider how great this man was, to whom even the patriarch Abraham gave a tenth of the spoils. And indeed, those who are the sons of Levi, who receive the priesthood, have a commandment to receive tithes from the people according to the law, that is from their brethren, though they have come from the loins of Abraham; but he whose genealogy is not derived from them received tithes from Abraham and blessed him who had the promises. Now beyond all contradiction the lesser is blessed by the better. Here mortal men receive tithes, but there he receives of them, of whom it is witnessed that he lives. Even Levi, who receives tithes, paid tithes through Abraham, so to speak, for he was still in the loins of his father when Melchizedek met him. Therefore, if perfection were through the Levitical priesthood (for under it the people received the law), what further need was there that another priest should rise according to the order of Melchizedek, and not be called according to the order of Aaron? For the priesthood being changed, of necessity there is also a change of the law. For He of whom these things are spoken belongs to another tribe, from which no man has officiated at the altar. (Hebrews 7:1–13 NKJV)

The transference was from Melchizedek to Christ, not the Levites to modern-day pastors. And since the priesthood has changed—the Levitical being done away with—so has the law that governed the priesthood. The tithe was never meant to be a means to create guilt in people if they did not give to a religious organization. The tithe was for the priests, the tithe was for the poor, the tithe was for the widows and orphans, and the tithes were for the foreigners. In other words, the tithes were to manifest the righteousness toward people who had: 1. No inheritance (the priests), 2. No parents or spouses (orphans and widows), and 3. No land or country (foreigners).

Every third and sixth years, all the tithe of the produce would go to not only the priests but to the orphans, widows, strangers. Some consider this a second tithe. But regardless of its designation, it amplifies the purpose and function of the tithe beyond the priests (Deuteronomy 14 and 26).

The aforementioned prominent magazine article proposed three tithes: 1. The Levitical or sacred tithe, which was first given by Abraham to Melchizedek. They propose this tithe is still binding to all believers; 2. the tithe of feasts and; 3. the tithe to the poor. They propose that these three tithes are separate. I disagree. Sometimes the tithes were to be brought into the storehouse, and sometimes, the tithes were to be eaten at home, especially before the establishment of the storehouse.

However, the storehouse was the main place for storing the produce to be distributed to the priests, poor, orphans, and widows.

Bring all the tithe into the storehouse that there may be meat in my house. All the tithe—the tithe for the priests and Levites; the tithe of the grains; and the tithe for the poor, fatherless and widows—were to be brought into the one house.

Lessons

- The tithe was not just for the priest. It was for the widows, the orphans, and the strangers (foreigners).
- The tithe was to serve as a reminder in Israel of the continual need of justice toward those who did not have it.
- The tithe would manifest the righteousness of the nation.
- The tithe would serve as a continual reminder against corruption and selfishness.

CHAPTER 4

The Storehouse

Bring all the tithes into the storehouse, that there may
be food in My house, and try me now in this, says the
Lord of hosts, If I will not open for you the windows of
heaven and pour you out such blessing that there will
not be room enough to receive it.

—Malachi 3:10 NKJV

The Bible is a very dangerous book. It is dangerous because while
it possesses the power to free people, it also possesses the power to
bind people. The scriptures can be used for good or for ill. How we
understand the Bible is critical to how we believe. How we have been
taught the Bible is critical to how we understand it. Many have been
taught to understand the scriptures based on a proof-text methodology.

Proof-text methodology is when a person or a church holds a position
or belief on a topic and uses scripture to support their stated position,
even when the text used is not speaking about the issue in the way they
are applying it. For example, during the days of slavery, slave-owners
would justify the system of slavery and the treatment of slaves by using
the Bible and pointing to scriptures such as, "slaves obey your masters,"
as proof that the heinous system was approved by G_d. Or many have
been burdened with guilt by churches that use the text, "G_d hates
divorce," as the basis for staying in abusive and unbearable marriages,

as though, "G_d loves abuse," if it happens in the marriage as the alternative. Malachi 3:10 has been used in such a way.

Malachi does not bring the issue of tithing into view until he first brings Israel's ill-treatment of the poor, the stranger, and the widow into view. The context of bringing the tithe into the storehouse is a judgment against Israel; the Levites are corrupt, and G_d will purify them. Israel has forgotten the poor and needy, but G_d will bring judgment on those who exploit wages and turn against the orphans, strangers, and widows. These are the groups outlined in Deuteronomy 14 that were supposed to be blessed by the tithe. In not returning the tithe, they neglected the needy. In not returning the tithe, corruption existed in the priesthood. Thus, they were cursed with a curse.

The call to bring the tithe into the storehouse was a call to repentance. It was a call to right wrongs. Why did they need to bring it into the storehouse? The storehouse was part of the temple. The temple was not the church as we think of church. The temple was where all the resources of Israel resided. It was the center of Israel's worship. And it was the center of Israel's banking system and money exchange. It was the center of Israel's judicial system. Therefore, the question is, what is the temple today? Is the temple the church? Is it the conference or union in Adventism? Is it the Vatican in Catholicism? What religious body represents the holiness of goods that we are to give, that is, the storehouse?

The Old Testament establishes the principle of type-antitype. This means that people and objects are used to represent Christ. Scriptures declare in Luke 24:27, "and beginning at Moses and all the Prophets, He expounded to them in all the scriptures the things concerning Himself." In John 5:39, Jesus declared to the Pharisees, "you search the scriptures, for in them you think you have eternal life; and these are they that testify of Me." The scriptures that Jesus referred to is what we call the Old Testament. The Old Testament testifies of Christ.

In the Old Testament, individuals beginning with Adam, Noah, Abraham, Joseph, Moses, and David all are types of Christs. But not only are people types of Christs. Objects such as the ark and the threshing floor are as well. Each of these objects finds its reality and true meaning in Christ. Thus, in addition to these, the temple represents Christ and the storehouse in particular.

In one of Jesus's encounters with the Pharisees after He cleansed the temple, they asked Him what sign He would show them that He had the authority to do these things? Jesus declared that if they destroyed this temple, He would raise it up in three days. They thought He was referring to the temple built by Solomon and then Zerubbabel, but He was speaking of His body. Jesus claimed that the temple they worshipped was a symbol pointing to Him.

Apostle Paul takes it further. What had been a mystery and declared by the apostles and prophets is that we are partakers in Christ. All that we need, all that we believe, the entire economy of our salvation is to be found in Christ, just as all that Israel would need would be found in the temple. Christ is our temple. Christ is our storehouse.

When the Israelites brought their tithe into the storehouse, it meant that their righteousness was a result of the sacrifice the Messiah would make and that all their goodness must be found in Him. Bringing the tithe into the storehouse was not a ritual. It was a substantive reality to maintain human dignity. G_d did not require Israelites to make sacrifices like the unbelieving nations that did so to appease their gods. The tithe was to keep the image of G_d uplifted in humanity. The fact that they had neglected the poor, the stranger, and the widow and the fact that the priests had become corrupt necessitated a call to holiness. This call was made by imploring Israel to return the tithes to the storehouse. When they would not return the tithes, they were robbing G_d. But how can you rob G_d who owns everything? What can man take from G_d? Does G_d need man's money? Did He not say, "if I were hungry, I would not tell you"? Did He not declare that "the cattle upon a thousand hills are mine"? Was Malachi declaring that man was robbing G_d of money? Absolutely not!

Man was robbing G_d of His connection with His creation: nature and humanity. Man was robbing G_d of His image. Wherein have we robbed you? You have robbed me in tithes and offerings. Bring all the tithes into the storehouse. The storehouse was a part of the temple where the resources were kept. It was the place that would provide for all Israel. When the tithes were withheld, all Israel suffered. When the tithes were returned faithfully, the poor, needy, strangers, widows, priests, and all of Israel benefitted.

A promise was made regarding faithfulness. G_d declared that He would open the windows of heaven and pour out a blessing that there would not be room enough to receive it. Today, this text is taught in an individualistic context. If you return your tithes, G_d will bless you. The scripture in Malachi is not addressed to an individual. It is addressed to the nation. The Jewish people were to bring their tithe into the storehouse so the nation would be blessed. Thus, the blessings He promised that He would pour out would be on the nation, not the individual. Why? Because an individual can be blessed while the nation is suffering, but if the nation is blessed, so are its people. What is this blessing? What does He mean when He says He would open the windows of heaven?

The window of heaven is a reference back to Genesis 8, when the flood came upon the earth, and the windows of heaven were eventually stopped. G_d gives provision by not providing bread but by providing grain. He provides grain by providing rain. Thus, when He declared that He would open the windows of heaven when Israel returned faithfully, He was saying that Israel's grain would not run out. Therefore, Israel's means to provide for the needy would not run out because He would not allow drought in the land. All these practices in the Old Testament would have their fulfillment in Christ.

Christ is the storehouse by which His people deposit their righteousness in Him. They do not store up for themselves but are benefitted to be a blessing to others. In a tangible way, the followers of Christ who bring their holiness to Him because it was derived of Him have access to every spiritual blessing as it is in Christ. These blessings allow the believers to grow like stall-fatted calves and trample the wicked. These blessings allow relationships to be repaired so that the hearts of the fathers will turn to their children and the hearts of the children to their fathers.

The storehouse is not a church, conference office, union office, or any organizational structure. The storehouse was a part of the temple of G_d in Israel, where His name was to be made known to all the nations. This type met its antitype in the coming of Yashua Hamashiach, Jesus the Christ.

During Jesus's public ministry, He was confronted daily by His enemies, the Scribes, Pharisees, and Herodians. The Pharisees upheld the orthodox teaching of Judaism and levied the accusation against Christ that He was doing away with the law of Moses. In the same way, some who are reading this may be struggling because they feel it undermines what they have been taught of scripture. I hope it does undermine what has been taught. I hope that quoting scripture on Saturday or Sunday morning that robbed the people of the true meaning of the text would confront your understanding. The Pharisees upheld practices that, practiced in isolation or for individual purposes, made people think they were holy. People engaged in giving that they might be seen by others. They would tithe of mint and anise and cumin. They would present themselves as holy in the eyes of the people by making spectacles of what they would give. It was all for show, and the people were gullible to believe. But Christ saw past their charade and declared that they had forsaken the weightier matters of the law: justice, mercy, and forgiveness.

Today's church has continued this error. They have made the giving of tithe a mark of organizational faithfulness rather than its symbol of righteousness. They have made giving of tithe a means to individual financial blessing rather than the uplifting of a downtrodden community. And in the same way, the beneficiaries of the tithe payers, the clergy, are more interested in how many suits they have rather than relieving the suffering. But there is hope. Today you may deposit your righteousness in the true storehouse so that withdrawals may be made from Him who is the width and length and depth and height of the love of G_d.

Lessons

- The storehouse was a type of Christ. It is not a church or a conference. The early church never considered the feet of the apostles as the new storehouse.
- Teaching that the storehouse represented anything or anyone other than Christ robs Him as being the source of our faith and the root of our righteousness.
- The storehouse was that part of the temple where resources were gathered and kept for the benefit of the people.
- Teaching that tithes is simply money to be put in a basket in a church or conference reduces the sacrifice of Christ and the shedding of His blood as the need of G_d to receive our money. This is a grievous lie.

CHAPTER 5

The Fulfillment of the Tithes

> Therefore, if perfection were through the Levitical priesthood (for under it the people received the law), what further need was there that another priest should arise according to the order of Melchizedek, and not be called according to the order of Aaron? For the priesthood being changed, of necessity there is also a change of the law. For He of whom these things are spoken belongs to another tribe, from which no man has officiated at the altar.
>
> —Hebrews 7:11–13 NKJV

In almost every Christian church, on any given Saturday or Sunday, the collection of tithes and offerings is a critical part of the liturgy. Many use Malachi 3 in a manner that it has become, not only tradition, but a sacrament of belief. To assume or presume that tithing is not an obligatory practice for the believer is anathema, and that person may even be considered a heretic. But is this the case?

Hebrews 7, in general, and Hebrews 7:11–13 manifest that there was a change in the priesthood. Even though the priesthood of Melchizedek came before the Levitical priesthood, it was the Levitical priesthood that would "point to" the Messiah and His work. The Levitical priesthood was not eternal and is not practiced by those who are followers of Jesus the Christ. That Levitical laws incorporated practices that would point to the coming Messiah does not establish eternal practices.

The book of Hebrews teaches that if perfection came through this system, it would not have been needed to establish another system. The move away from the Levitical system is not a move away from Israel. It is not a rejection of the system that was followed for nearly four thousand years. The book of Hebrews simply teaches that it has fulfilled its purpose, and now that the true sacrifice has been offered, there is no need for the shadow. Just as Melchizedek gave the bread and wine, Christ gave His body and blood. We have a greater High Priest who does not have to offer Himself up daily but once for all. And as Abram returned a tenth of the spoil to Melchizedek as a symbol of the righteousness that is returned on behalf of the sacrifice, believers must not give a shadow of the righteousness but the real. No longer is 10 percent required. Rather, we must give 100 percent.

If the priesthood has been changed, if the Levitical priesthood has been done away with, then there is of necessity a change of the law. There are no Levitical priests operating as followers of the Christ today. If we still operate under the Levitical order, then we declare that Christ has not come. But Christ has come, and He did not come from the tribe of Levi. Rather, He came from the tribe of Judah, which did not belong to the priesthood. If Christ did not have to come from the Levitical priesthood, it is because the Levitical priesthood and the law were tutors to point to Christ. One system pointed us *to* Christ. The other system has drawn us to be *in* Christ.

> For on the one hand there is an annulling of the former commandment because of its weakness and unprofitableness, for the law made nothing perfect; on the other hand, there is the bringing in of a better hope, through which we draw near to G_d. (Hebrews 11:18, 19)

If this is true, then the tithing system falls under the ceremonial system. And even if you believe it does not fall under the ceremonial system, it is in the same category as circumcision.

These are not light issues. When someone's beliefs are challenged, he may experience a fight-or-flight response. When it comes to religion, people most often fight. Most of the New Testament reveals the fight between the Israel nation and those Jews who became followers of Christ and had a new understanding of what He fulfilled. The Jewish leaders sought to kill, imprison, and beat the followers of the way to keep control of the people. That is why this is such a major issue. Money has power over the lives of people, and those who control the spiritual consciences of the people thereby control their lives. Not a few will see this book as a threat to their belief systems instead of an amazing opportunity for people to be freed by truth. Anyone who deems to use this book as an excuse to no longer give to the cause of Christ is revealing his or her character and will never give a truly faithful tithe or offering.

We no longer must sacrifice bulls or goats; that system has been done away with. However, the principle of sacrifice remains. Paul wrote, "Present your bodies a living sacrifice, holy and acceptable unto G_d which is your reasonable service. Circumcision of a man's reproductive parts is no longer required to be done on the 8th day after his birth. However, circumcision of the heart is still required by those who fall under the blood of Christ.

We cannot be bipolar or schizophrenic in our beliefs. On one side, many in Christianity promote women to be ordained as pastors, and in the same breath, declare that the tithe is still obligatory. They use the Word of G_d to make their own systems according to their own rules. Let us not turn the Word of G_d into our image.

The *Seventh-Day Adventist Commentary*, volume 8, pages 1127 and 1128, recognizes that the tithe established by Abram was incorporated into the Levitical system. However, it reads,

The command to pay tithes is not explicitly restated by any of the NT writers. But since Abraham, as a matter of course, paid tithe centuries before the formulation of the Levitical code, and that the principle of tithe paying was implicit even before man sinned, it is evident that the principle and practice of tithe paying existed long before the Levitical system came into being and was not peculiar to it. Therefore, the obligation to pay tithe was not automatically waived when the Levitical code became inoperative at the cross. Our Lord's admonition on Mt. 23:23 constitutes tacit approval, though not an explicit command for tithe paying.

This is problematic on several levels.

The first problem is that Abram returned a tithe of the spoils, not a tithe of his income. To use Abram as the basis for continual returning of tithe is contrary at best and disingenuous at worst to the scriptures, especially in the book of Hebrews. The book of Hebrews acknowledges the return of tithe by Abram to Melchizedek, and at the same time, promotes the dissolution of returning the tithes on a basis of any type of priesthood.

The second problem with this stated position is that it upholds that because tithe was practiced before the formulation of the Levitical code means it is a perpetual covenant. It states that tithe paying was implicit before man sinned. I know of no such practice before man's sin. The fact of the matter is that almost every practice in the Levitical laws existed prior to it being codified. Moses codified the law, but he did not establish the law. Moses is recognized for the codification of the law, not the creation of the law. Prior to the law being codified under Moses, circumcision was established as a perpetual covenant. This law of circumcision was believed to be continued even after the cross. This was a point of contention for even those who accepted Christ. Did they still need to be circumcised? A practice existing prior to its codification in the Levitical system in no way speaks to its perpetual practice after the cross. The sacrifice of animals existed prior to its codification under

Moses; Jesus is the lamb slain from the foundation of the earth, but these two truths do not maintain the reality of animal sacrifices as a requirement for believers.

The third problem posed by the stated position in the commentary is that it uses Jesus's comment in Matthew 23:23 as tacit proof for returning tithe up to this day. Jesus's comment in Matthew 23 is prior to the cross. In all His dealings, Jesus always upheld the law. He told the lepers to show themselves to the priest even though their healing was complete. In Matthew 23, He declared seven woes upon the Pharisees and scribes because He deemed them hypocrites. He declared that they paid tithe of mint and anise and cumin but negated the weightier matters of the law. Was He making a statement regarding the perpetuity of the tithe? Absolutely not!

If we extrapolate the text, the position of three tithes loses credibility. This is not to say that there weren't three different functions for the tithes. To use Matthew 23 to uphold the continuity of the text means that the tithe of grain is still applicable. It is the tithe of the land and grain that Jesus refers to mint, anise, and cumin. But as mentioned earlier, they neglected the weightier matters of the law. In Malachi, Israel and its leaders forgot the poor, needy, and the stranger. This was manifest and highlighted in the fact that as a nation, they were not bringing their goods to the storehouse. In Matthew 23, Jesus acknowledged that they returned a tithe and still neglected justice and righteousness.

Hebrews chapter 7, probably more than any pericope of scripture, outlines the reason for the dissolution of tithes. As we already established, the tithe was a symbol of righteousness. This symbol was established just as Melchizedek was a symbol of Christ, and bread and wine are symbols of His body and blood. Our Savior did not die so that He could receive man's money. He died so that man might indeed fulfill the function and purpose originally intended by his Maker.

The law was meant to be a schoolmaster or tutor to sinful man. It could not produce righteousness in and of itself. Thus, the writer of Hebrews systematically establishes that righteousness is only found in Christ. The system that was established to point to the Messiah made no one righteous in that it was not perfect.

Therefore, those who ministered according to that system have ceased. There is no more priesthood according to the Aaronic order or the Levitical order. But here's the key:

> Therefore if perfection were through the Levitical priesthood (for under it the people received the law), what further need was there that another priest should rise according to the order of Melchizedek, and not be called according to the order of Aaron? For the priesthood being changed, of necessity there is also change of the law. (Hebrews 7:11–13)

Did you get it? The former priesthood changed, and with it, the law that governed that system. But what is the change, and what governs people of G_d's giving today?

Lessons

- There is a change in the law governing the priesthood. The Levitical priesthood found its fulfillment in Christ. The shadow is no longer the focus. The real has arrived.
- Tithes represented the righteousness that was required as a response to the sacrifice of Christ. Robbing the storehouse of tithes was a symbol of robbing Christ of the righteous response to His sacrifice.
- Jesus's reference to tithes in Matthew 23:23 cannot be credibly used as a premise for the continuation of tithes.

CHAPTER 6

The New Covenant

In that He says, "A new covenant," He has made the first obsolete. Now what is becoming obsolete and growing old is ready to vanish away.

—Hebrews 8:13 NKJV

There are many who declare the old covenant is done away with, and we are under the new covenant. Still, there are others who declare what was written in the Old Testament is still binding for Christians to follow. The denomination you belong to probably informs your position on this matter. However, allow me to challenge both positions.

There is no mention of an "old covenant" in all the Bible. Be careful of adopting and debating words and terms that are not in the scriptures. Yes, the "old" is implied in Hebrews when compared to the establishment of a new covenant. On further scrutiny, the terms may be misleading. Not only is the new covenant referred to as "new," it is referenced as a "better covenant" established on better promises and called an "everlasting covenant." The old covenant" is referenced as the "first covenant."

Though there is no mention of an old covenant in the Old Testament, it mentions several covenants. Thus, the old covenant is not one covenant but the compilation of all the covenants in the Old Testament. More specifically, it refers to eight primary covenants:

- The Edenic covenant
- The Adamic covenant
- The Noahic covenant
- The Abrahamic covenant
- The Mosaic covenant
- The Aaronic covenant
- The Davidic covenant
- The Solomonic covenant.

It is also interesting that each covenant was established or ratified by a symbol for the covenant.

The Edenic Covenant

The Edenic covenant is a reference to the promise that G_d made to Adam when He placed him in the garden of Eden. It would be his home and ratified by the dominion he would possess over the animals of the earth, sea, and air. This dominion of his home was also symbolized in his naming of the animals. Whoever names another has dominion over what it has named. Parents name their children to represent the responsibilities they have toward their children. G_d gives His people a new name representing His rulership over their lives.

The Edenic covenant is a promise that man will forever have a home. What a message during these days of homelessness! What a promise!

However, with the promise comes the responsibility of man to till the ground. Another symbol of the Edenic covenant was the work man was to engage in. Work is not a result of sin. Work is a symbol of divining favor and divine character. When you witness someone who doesn't work, it means the person manifests no dominion, and the individual's home is in jeopardy. This covenant would be threatened after sin as man would have to work by the sweat of his brow, and his dominion would be challenged.

The Adamic Covenant

G_d established the Adamic covenant with Adam (male and female) to be fruitful and multiply. It is the covenant of duplication. Man would procreate, create on behalf of G_d, and the sexual relationship would be defined as holy between male and female. Adam, the Son of G_d, would create man in his likeness. As long as he was connected to G_d, his procreation would also be in the likeness of G_d. The symbol established for this relationship was marriage.

This covenant would also be threatened by sin's entrance and man's disobedience to G_d. The marriage relationship would be characterized by competition rather than collaborative cooperation. The sexual relationship would go beyond marriage faithfulness and explore beyond male and female intimacy. It is through this covenant that the promise of a seed was made, and that salvation would come through not only the grace of G_d but through the womb of a woman.

The Noahic Covenant

The Noahic covenant is one of renewal established between G_d and Noah. Under this covenant, man began to consume for pleasure that which he was to have dominion over. Distinction between clean and unclean animals were made for land, sea, and air. Unfortunately, these distinctions did not curb man's appetite, and G_d decided to destroy the earth, except for Noah and those who would follow his example. Even Noah's handling of the fruit of the vine showed the continuation of this perversion when released from the ark. G_d symbolized His promise not to destroy the earth after this manner again with the symbol of the rainbow. Despite man's continual devolution into consuming other living creatures, G_d has maintained this covenant.

In addition to the rainbow symbol, the Noahic covenant uses the ark to symbolize G_d's continual protection in His judgment of man. Many have used the ark as a symbol of the church: Come into the ark of safety. This is inaccurate. The ark is a symbol of Christ. Everyone has to build the ark for themselves and their families (Hebrews 11:7). The church was "in" the ark. Noah and his family, which would be the progenitors of both Jews and Gentiles, are symbolized by the clean and unclean animals (Acts 10). In each covenant, an aspect of the gospel was symbolized and testified.

Abrahamic Covenant

The Abrahamic covenant established G_d's call upon the imperfect and the sacrifice that would come through that call. The themes of, "come out of her," and Babylon fall under the Abrahamic covenant. It is also through this covenant that man's weakness would be revealed in choosing a man and woman who could not reproduce on their own power. The power of G_d would be made manifest in that which was weak and impotent in and of itself.

The Abrahamic covenant was symbolized by three symbols: circumcision, sacrifice, and tithe. Circumcision was chosen since it was through the sexual relationship that the Messiah would appear. Sacrifice (Genesis 15) because it symbolized what the Messiah would offer and the payment in blood. The tithe was established as a response to the sacrifice of the Messiah (Genesis 14).

Through the Abrahamic covenant, the promise of a blessing to all the families of the earth was made. Abraham is not only the father of the Jews. He is the father of the faithful of all families of the earth. This was fulfilled through not only the birth of Isaac, who represented the child of promise, but also through his other sons.

The Mosaic Covenant

It is under the Mosaic covenant that the previous covenants and the laws that governed them were codified. The sexual relationships of humanity, the sacrificial system, the tithe system, the practice of circumcision, the laws governing man's consumption of other living creatures, all these found their codifications under the Mosaic covenant. Unfortunately, many teach and preach as though these aspects began under Moses. They did not. G_d used Moses to call a people as a fulfillment of a promise He made to Abraham. These people were to stand in juxtaposition to the other nations to show the grace and glory of G_d. The Mosaic covenant used various symbols to represent the principles of the covenant. No symbol under the Mosaic covenant is greater than the symbol of the sanctuary.

It is through the symbol of the sanctuary that G_d would convey the principle of His desire not only to dwell among man but to dwell in man. The sanctuary symbol is carried through the time of the appearance of the Messiah and is the highlighted in David's desire to build a temple for the Lord.

Aaronic Covenant

The Aaronic covenant, named after Moses's brother, established two primary functions: First, it established the methodology of how G_d gave a message to a prophet and used the prophet as a mouthpiece. G_d told Moses that he would be G_d to Pharaoh, and Aaron would be His mouthpiece. G_d will not be seen, but His message would still go forth.

The covenant also established the aspect of mediation and intercession of the priesthood. The priests would intercede on behalf of the people to G_d, and the people of G_d would be mediators and intercessors for the nations. This is the basis of the priesthood of all beliefs.

The primary symbol of this covenant was the rod. The rod was not simply a piece of stick. The rod was the emblem for each family. The name of the head of the family was written on each rod and the totem that represented each family. Aaron's rod was chosen to be over all the house of Levi. His rod was selected over all the other houses against those who rebelled against G_d. Thus, the rod also represented truth and correction.

A rod or a branch broken off from the tree is a dead stick. However, Aaron's rod came to life when it turned into a snake and devoured the rods of the Egyptian magicians. It was Aaron's rod that was placed in the Most holy tabernacle of meeting where it budded anew. This gave testimony to the reality of that which was dead finds life anew when connected to the presence of G_d.

Davidic Covenant

The Davidic covenant was established when Israel moved away from a theocracy and established a monarchy. G_d used this transition to establish the principle of His everlasting throne. The Davidic covenant established the principle that the throne of David would be established forever. Through this covenant. G_d's promise of land, descendants, and blessings would be assured.

David is chosen in direct contradiction to the people of G_d. The people chose Saul of the tribe of Benjamin, from the family of Kis. He was the tallest and the best looking. But his throne would represent the failing of humanity that always leans toward external features. G_d chose David, a young man, who his mother and father didn't deem worthy of mention when Samuel was directed to the house of Jesse. The Davidic covenant, in a deep and meaningful way, is a message to all those who are rejected.

The main symbol for this covenant is a throne. G_d would establish a throne forever. And the people would be protected by the presence of an enduring king.

Solomonic Covenant

The Solomonic covenant is a continuation and fulfillment of the Davidic covenant. David wanted to build a "house" temple for G_d so that He may dwell with His people. Sound familiar? David was not allowed to build the temple, but he made all the provisions necessary for Solomon to complete it.

This covenant provides several insights in to the blessings and promises of G_d. It reveals that G_d once again chooses the one who should receive nothing. Solomon should not have been born. He was birthed by Bathsheba, who was another man's wife. His father, David, broke his connection to G_d, yet we see the grace and mercy of G_d in His choice of Solomon.

The Solomonic covenant is also a warning. Even though one may do great exploits for G_d and build symbols to Him, nothing replaces an abiding humility and distrust of self. While Solomon chose wisdom and the presence of G_d in his early years, there is danger that man can confuse trusting in G_d and trusting in self.

The enduring symbol in this covenant is the temple of G_d. The building followed the pattern of the Mosaic sanctuary but also added extensions to a greater degree. Instead of being satisfied with building the temple of G_d, Solomon also built his own house. The message is simple: G_d will not dwell in two houses. We can do things that make us appear to be with G_d, while at the same time, build things that serve ourselves.

All these covenants contained promises, conditions, and failures of those conditions. Does this mean that all of them are irrelevant? Does this mean they did not fulfill their purposes? Does this mean the Old Testament/covenant was a waste of time? G_d forbid. The Old covenant/Testament was never dependent on man to fulfill the conditions. As a matter of fact, G_d patiently dealt with man to reveal that he could not meet the conditions of the covenants. Man did not—and in many respects, still does not—understand the exceeding sinfulness of sin. However, the purpose of the covenants was to point to the One who would come and meet the conditions of the covenants.

While the Edenic home was lost, Christ has forever secured our eternal home. Where the Adams fell, the last Adam stood true. Where Noah got drunk and perpetuated man's misuse of his dominion, Christ came and subjected the elements to Himself. Where Abraham lied and laid with Hagar, Christ fulfilled the symbol of the tithe by not only being our bread and wine but by being our tithe and fulfilling righteousness. Where Moses was a murderer and became frustrated with the people, Christ brought life, fulfilled the law, and maintains patient endurance for His people. Where Aaron and the Levites and their descendants served themselves and sought to please the people, Christ came and did the will of His Father, and He forever lives to make intercessions for His people. And where David and Solomon failed, Christ has established His throne and temple forever.

In Galatians, Paul wrote, "the law was our schoolmaster to bring us to Christ." There is a difference between that which is done away with and that which is fulfilled. The new covenant fulfills the eight covenants of the Old Testament. The new covenant replaced the previous covenants in that it is found in a person, namely, Jesus the Messiah. Christ is our Eden; Christ is our Adam; Christ is our rainbow; Christ is our Melchizedek; Christ is our tithe; Christ is our law; Christ is our rod; Christ is our throne, and Christ is our temple! He who has the Son has life, and anyone who does not have the Son does not have life.

Lessons

- The old covenant is a compilation of the covenants in the Old Testament.
- The old covenant was never meant to be everlasting. It was meant to point to Christ and His salvific work.

- If any of the eight covenants listed are still binding, it negates the sacrifice of Christ.
- Tithing has the same significance as circumcision. They both represent a greater lesson than their temporal physical applications.

CHAPTER 7

The Widow's Mite

Now Jesus sat opposite the treasury and saw how the people put money into the treasury. And many who were rich put in much. Then one poor widow came and threw in two mites, which makes a quadrans. So, he called His disciples to Himself and said to them, Assuredly, I say to you that this poor widow has put in more than all those who have given to the treasury; for they all put in out of their abundance, but she out of her poverty put in all she had, her whole livelihood.

—Mark 12:41–44 NKJV

Religion is a difficult thing. It presents the best of people and the worst of people. Religion is supposed to represent G_d, but it is not G_d. Religion is run by man, and since it is run by man, it is susceptible to all the foibles of man: nepotism, favoritism toward friends, misappropriation of funds, political agendas in the name of G_d, corruption disguised in prayer, political systems with votes disguised as G_d's leading, narcissistic leaders, unfaithful members. The list can go on and on. What is sad is that some people are impacted by aspects of religion that leave them unaware, unassuming, and at the whims of nefarious minds, wolves in sheep clothing. The desire of those to please G_d is often subjected to the desire of those to please themselves.

The story of the widow's mite displayed a great tragedy taking place. However, what was a tragedy has been turned into a message that perpetrates a fraud in many churches today. Since I was a child—and even now, as an adult—I have heard the message of the widow's mite preached as a principle of giving your all. Even though the church (temple) was full of crooks, the widow gave her all because she was giving to G_d, and Jesus called His disciples to recognize what the widow had done. This is how misinterpreting a biblical text can take on a life of its own. It sounds good. Great stewardship message. But it's a lie to the context of the story and the reason Jesus called His disciples' attention to this unnamed widow. Jesus is about to teach one of His final lessons during the week before His crucifixion.

The scribes and Pharisees had done their best to trap Jesus in His words. They sought every opportunity to turn the people away from Him because He was a threat to their control of the people. Those who control the minds of the people ultimately control their finances and their understandings of giving to G_d. The scribes and Pharisees brought up the issue of money when they asked Him about paying taxes to Caesar. They opened the door to their own hypocrisy, which led to Jesus's famous seven "woes" pronounced on these religious leaders. However, he needed to drive the message home to His disciples. Thus, Jesus made His way to the treasury of the temple. On this, His last day in the temple, He made His way to the place that reveals the most about a person's righteous actions.

Jesus positioned Himself and watched the show the Pharisees put on for those in the audience of their giving. It is believed that when individuals gave significant amounts to the treasury, an announcement would be made, bringing more attention to the giver. As they gave, Jesus watched *how* they gave, not *what* they gave. How they gave revealed the true aspects of their giving. The Pharisees gave for show hidden behind false piety. John 12 highlights this reality:

> Nevertheless, even among the rulers many believed in
> Him, but because of the Pharisees they did not confess

Him, lest they should be put out of the synagogue; for they loved the praise of men more than the praise of G_ d. (John 14:42 NKJV)

As the show commenced, and the people gloried in those who gave substantial amounts of money, someone caught the attention of the Master. An unknown was about to break the pattern of giving. An elderly woman of no significance was about to dare to mix her measly offering with the substantive offerings of those who considered themselves significant. Not only was she a woman, she was a widow. She walked up and "threw" her money into the treasury. Now, she had three strikes against her: She was a woman, she was poor, and she was a widow. Based on the original intent of the system, she should not have given anything to the treasury. The treasury should have given to her.

Established in previous chapters, the tithes were to go to the priests, the widows, the orphans, and the strangers. It was to be a blessing to those who had no inheritance, no spouse, no parents, and no country. But the scribes and Pharisees had pilfered widows. Jesus declared in Mark 12:38–40:

Then He said to them in His teaching, Beware of the Scribes, who desire to go around in long robes, love greetings in the marketplaces, the best seats in the synagogues, and the best places at the feasts, who devour widows' houses, and for a pretense make long prayers. These will receive greater condemnation. (Mark 12:38 NKJV)

The scribes, as well as the Pharisees, were known to take advantage of widows who unknowingly signed away their houses usually left behind by their deceased spouse. The system that was meant to take care of these individuals now took advantage of them. Jesus was mesmerized and took the opportunity to teach His disciples a critical lesson.

He called them over, and yes, Judas was there. It's amazing that a lesson could be made so plain, but because of where one's heart is, someone missed the opportunity for transformation. As the disciples came to Him and observed the scribes, Pharisees, and the widow, Jesus declared that the widow had given more than everyone else because, while they gave out of their excesses, she gave out of her poverty. By itself, it sounds like Jesus was commending the widow. But no! It was not so much a commendation to the widow as it was a condemnation of the scribes and Pharisees. It was a condemnation of what the system had become.

The sanctuary treasury system became a system through which poor people ministered to the rich. It became a system that flouted and touted those who gave out of their abundance, while they did not lift a finger to relieve the suffering of the poor. It had become a system that one could use to elevate their own causes and advance self-promotion based on the appearance of giving much. The widow threw her money in, not from a sense of faithfulness, but from a sense of obligation taught by the Pharisees to appease G_d. G_d would be appeased while they appropriated the widow's offering. She gave, not to be recognized by man, but because if she didn't give, G_d would be displeased. She didn't realize that even what she had been taught about G_d was a perversion.

She went home wondering how she would eat. She gave to G_d wondering if she would be able to afford rent, since she had lost her home to the Pharisees. She gave to G_d wondering how she would afford her medication for her arthritis, her chronic disease, and her Roman taxes, let alone the sanctuary tax. When a system that was established to protect the marginalized turns into a system that benefits the affluent, you can rest assured that G_d is not in it. Jesus said to His disciples, "look at this poor widow." He wanted His disciples to see the contrast between the leadership of the temple and the people of the temple so that they would never allow themselves to become like the scribes and Pharisees.

How much of the church budget is spent on the orphans and the widows? When the senior citizen is taking the bus or train to the church, what does she leave with? Does she leave with more or less than when she came? Does the church even know about her living conditions? Does the church know what she must pay for medical expenses? While guest speakers now ask for obnoxious amounts of money to speak at churches, and musicians feel slighted if they are not paid according to their talents, who is giving voice to the widows in board and business meetings? Who is giving voice to foster children? Are they even on the agenda? They are on the agenda of heaven. And the all-seeing eye of G_d takes note of the religiosity of man and the burden of the neglected.

Many like to make false applications. They think the temple is equivalent to the church, priests are equivalent to pastors, the most holy place is the pulpit, and the holy place is where the congregation sits. Such pedantic applications are what keep many of our people religious hostages. The temple in Jesus's day was not solely religious. The temple was economic. The temple was the center of Israel's banking system and where loans were made and taxes collected. The temple represented Israel's Wall Street. And Jesus attacked the center of Israel's economy. He did not attack it because of the money changers or dove sellers but because of abusive financial practices against the poor that benefitted the rich. Today, the widows still contribute their mite because of their might! But some will have to pay a much higher price for this tragedy and travesty.

Lessons

- The widow gave to take care of a system that was originally designed to take care of her.
- Jesus's bringing attention to the widow's mite was not a commendation of her giving. He called His disciples for the express purpose of showing them how not to be like the Pharisees and the religious leaders. Jesus wasn't commending the widow; He was condemning the religious leaders.
- A system that causes people to give from their livelihoods is not a system that strengthens faith. It is a system that places undue burdens on the people.

CHAPTER 8

Ananias and Sapphira

Nor was there any among them who lacked; for all who were possessors of lands or houses sold them and brought the proceeds of the things that were sold and laid them at the apostles' feet; and they distributed to each as anyone had need.

—Acts 4:34, 35 NKJV

The early church was a tight-knit group of 120 believers, which included 11 of the original apostles. The Holy Spirit had fallen, and the small group that was considered just a new sect knew they had power available to them to preach the gospel of the risen Christ. In one day, they had grown to over three thousand believers in the Christ. The family of heaven was now a reality to the church on earth. The mystery that had been hidden in ages past was now the reality found in the crucified and risen Christ. And they went forward with power.

The believers had the task of giving a message of a risen Christ to a Roman culture that deemed it illegal to claim a king other than Caesar. The Jewish nation had forfeited being the special people of G_d when they rejected the Messiah and claimed Caesar as their king. This newly forged movement had to reach their own people with a new interpretation and application of the scriptures. They had to reach Gentiles with this newfound understanding that would mean an allegiance to someone greater and other than Caesar. And they had to facilitate the growth and care of the movement through financial means.

Hope was experienced when many rich members of the Jewish economy accepted the message of Jesus the Christ. In His death, Joseph of Arimathea and Nicodemus stepped forward. The system, however, would not and could not be dependent just on the rich. Everyone had to contribute to the cause of Christ, the furtherance of the gospel, and the care of the believers. These early believers would no longer bring their tithes and offerings to the temple, even though they would still attend the temple for prayers and for teaching the scriptures considering the Christ.

The system would be simple enough: Let each give based on a vow to the Lord that would be made not out of necessity or compulsion. As the Holy Spirit moved upon the people of G_d, many sold their homes and laid the proceeds at the feet of the apostles. The apostles then distributed them based on the needs of the community and the furtherance of the gospel. Later, when the apostle Paul would be an instrument to reach the Gentiles, offerings would be collected to support the causes in different areas. However, the people's first responsibilities were to take care of those in their own communities.

The giving was of such a magnanimous spirit that great praise was heaped upon many early on. One such person was Joses Barnabas. His name would become well known in the early church and in the book of Acts as he would be instrumental in introducing the apostle Paul to the original eleven, as well as becoming Paul's missionary partner. Barnabas, the cousin of John Mark, who wrote the second gospel, was lauded and praised for his generosity. He sold his house and land and laid the proceeds at the feet of the apostle so that there would be no lack among the believers. But it is early on that the enemy of our souls seeks access to our hearts. Envy and jealousy are invisible spirits that damn the soul.

Amid the praises of the people, Ananias and his wife, Sapphira, decided to make a vow to sell their possessions and give to the new movement. However, their vow was not based on what Christ did for them. It was not based on the merits of the blood of our Savior or given out of love for the people and the uplifting of the community of believers. The reason they decided to sell their possessions was that they saw the praise people heaped upon Barnabas, and they desired the praise of men.

We see it in the entertainment industry and in church, the desire to be praised by men. We see it on the football field, and we see it in the pulpit. We see it on the basketball court, and we see it in the choir loft. And we see it on the "red carpet" and on the church carpet. The desire to be praised, the desire to be admired, the desire to be acknowledged by others is a motivating factor for many. Take the praise away, and a gloom settles over the hearts and minds of many. Social media has given the masses the platform to draw the praise of men. But this is not to be a factor in giving to G_d or to the cause of G_d.

Ananias and Sapphira chose to make a vow. They were not compelled by the apostles to do so; they were not under any obligation; The apostles did not hand out tithe and offering envelopes dictating how much the people needed to give. They laid before that early group and shared with them the need. The early church had an uphill battle. They had to battle the established religion of Judaism, with its intricate system and financial strength. And it also had to do this in the Roman Empire with an illegal message. How would they be supported financially? How would they advance the message? How would they protect their communities? They trusted the people to give. The people were encouraged to give not because it was compulsory or necessary. They gave based on a love for what Christ had done in their lives.

The leaven of jealousy and envy reared their ugly heads early in the church. As it so often happens, those who are under the sway of jealousy and envy rarely acknowledge it until they must. Jealousy and envy are forms of covetousness. How so? There was a desire to have what someone else was receiving. Covetousness takes many forms, but it is in essence the same. This is what happened with Israel.

The children of Israel had wandered forty years in the wilderness. Those over twenty years of age had died, and now they were going into the Promised Land. The walls of Jericho had fallen, and the people were instructed not to take anything for themselves. But Achan! Achan took what was forbidden, thereby threatening the presence of G_d among the people and the peace of the community. He was given opportunity after opportunity to confess, but he wouldn't. Even after his tribe was chosen, even after his clan was chosen, even after his family was chosen, Achan still didn't confess. It was only when he was pointed out that he admitted what he had done.

As it was with Israel, so it was with the early church. The spirits of self, greed, and praise found places in the hearts of believers. The husband-and-wife team decided together; they were unified in what they were doing. They made a vow to give the proceeds but chose to hold some back for themselves. In other words, they wanted to be praised for giving all while not giving all.

Ananias and Sapphira went through a process in selling their possessions. The ability to sell possessions in the Roman Empire meant that you were probably part of the equites, the highest level in a caste or class system in the Roman Empire. Many senators came from the equites level. To be part of this highest class, you owned horses, land, or jewelry. The equites were differentiated by assets. Higher ranks had privilege over lower ranks. Thus, to sell assets had a great impact on one's status in society. To sell possessions meant to lose prestige and opportunities. We may now begin to understand why Ananias and Sapphira decided to hold back a portion of the proceeds from the sale of their possessions. They thought they had found a way to give to the early movement of the early church while maintaining their status in the Roman Empire.

The selling of the possession may have taken time, but the confrontation was immediate. As Ananias came in among the believers and laid the possessions at the feet of the apostles, Peter immediately addressed the deception. Oh, if that were to take place in churches today. Did Peter know the going rate of selling possessions at that time? Had Peter read the Jerusalem Nasdaq report? Did the apostles keep up with the Judean stock market? Why did you lie to the Holy Spirit? In other words, why would you lie to the Spirit that oversees your conscience? Why would you lie to yourself? Why would you deceive yourself? You are certainly not deceiving us.

The church made no mandate to sell property. The church made no obligatory giving of tithe with another 5 percent offering. "Ananias, why have you conceived this thing in your heart?" No answer was ever recorded. On hearing the words, he died. About three hours after the young men of the church had taken out the body of Ananias, Sapphira came in with the same story. And got the same result as her husband. The issue is not money. The issue is righteous character. Money is just the medium by which righteousness and character are manifested.

How would you change if you became a multimillionaire? How often would you be seen in the house of G_d? How far away would you move from where you now live? How drastic would your friends change? Yes, money leads the heart. Tithes and offerings are not about money. The true giver understands this. Have you developed a righteous character because of the sacrifice of body and blood offered on your behalf?

Lessons

- Giving to G_d is not based on a 10 percent model to a temple system. Giving to G_d must be based on the value His followers place on His Son's sacrifice.
- The feet of the apostles began the transition from the storehouse of the temple.
- If you make a vow to G_d, you must keep that vow.
- Making a vow to give for the purpose of receiving recognition and praise will never be accepted by G_d. Instead, it will reveal itself for what it is.

- Giving is a decision of the heart and head that must be rooted in honest faith. Any aspect of a lie cannot be mixed with the blessings of G_d.
- The experiences of Ananias and Sapphira are lessons of the heart, not of the wallet or purse.

CHAPTER 9

The Giver

But this I say: He who sows sparingly will also reap sparingly, and he who sows bountifully will also reap bountifully. So let each one give as he purposes in his heart, not grudgingly or of necessity; for G_d loves a cheerful giver.

—2 Corinthians 9:6 NKJV

If you have gotten to this point of the book, you may be in one of two camps: (1) The author is saying we don't have to give anymore, or (2) The author is undermining the law of G_d because the Bible clearly states, "bring all the tithes into the storehouse." Both positions would be incorrect. If you believe you don't have to give to the cause of G_d while claiming to be a follower of G_d, that is cognitive dissonance. Seek help. If you think your obligation is to give 10 percent as mandatory from G_d, you don't understand the meaning of tithes and the position of the law in relation to salvation. This is not meant in a disrespectful way but as a result of being controlled by the teaching of colonial Christianity.

The Bible counsels many things regarding money and the obligation of the believer. The follower of G_d is challenged to live in the world while not being of the world. There is a balancing act that the disciple of the one G_d must navigate. Many who live in Western culture are inundated with the capitalistic ideology that the more you have, the better your life. The accumulation of wealth is used as a barometer of how well G_d has blessed you. However, if you lack financial resources, it is a sign that the blessings of G_d have not come your way. Money is more than money. Money affects self-image, self-worth, and value. Money makes people happy, and a lack of money can cause sadness and depression.

We will now consider two aspects regarding those who give to the cause of G_d: responsibility and attitude. In a capitalistic society, where pleasure and material gain often override sacrifice, how does the believer operate in a system that claims to follow G_d while operating against the kingdom of G_d? There are principles that should govern kingdom citizens. However, rarely are they taught in a meaningful way. For most people who attend church, the responsibility as it relates to money begins and ends with giving a faithful tithe and offering.

The Responsible Giver

It took me many years to learn the power of money and its psychological, emotional, and spiritual implications. Growing up in a single-parent home, you learn to go without while, at the same time, developing a desire for more. Learning to give to G_d and the church while living in a context of need is not easy. How much will we eat this week? Will we have to go on public assistance? Will we all be able to go to college? These are legitimate questions facing people with limited resources. The church I grew up attending did an excellent job of fostering the belief that we can accomplish anything. It pushed education and hard work, but principles and the power of money were not taught. This left many to navigate and balance giving money to the church while struggling at home. Of course, this turned in to a message of faith. If you fail to give to G_d (the church), it is because you lack faith and need to obey G_d. These are the psychological manipulations that take place by well-meaning people. But in many ways, they do more harm than good. Let us consider kingdom principles that will guide people in various contexts to uphold the teachings of G_d while being faithful to their families, communities, and churches.

Do Not Live beyond Your Means

This may seem almost impossible in a society that says you can have it all. You see people driving luxurious cars or living in nice homes, and it's natural to want these comforts too. We want the nice clothes and the ability to travel for happy vacations, where we can take pictures and post them on social media. The problem is these things are often done using credit, which brings interest.

There is an inability to give to the cause of G_d because many have bitten off more than they can chew. Many are drowning in debt because of the inability to wait. This is not an indictment. It is a call to reprioritize which kingdom we are really part of. A principle of the Word is, "owe no one anything except to love."

Work

This may seem obvious, but in Western culture, the desire for ease and comfort has replaced the principle of work. True work benefits the individual, the family, the community, and the world. To make decisions that only benefit self is not of the kingdom of G_d. The true disciple understands that the gifts and talents given by G_d are to be increased, and increase comes through usage. Whether your work is mostly physical or mental, it can only be improved on by expending energy in the aspect you choose. Video games, idleness, consumption of time without purpose are contrary to the kingdom. "If you don't work, you don't eat."

This is not a principle to be used against those who are qualified to work but are displaced due to racism, ageism, or sexism. This is not a principle against those who seek work but can't find work, or entrepreneurs who find themselves struggling. In a capitalist society that facilitates excess and consumerism, many laws are established that keep people poor. Many single parents must choose between working long hours and being away from their children while much of their paychecks go to child care. Senior citizens are limited in their work abilities while trying to afford rising housing prices. They battle with paying rent, buying food, or paying for health care. Those who do work find themselves with aging parents, which brings rising costs.

Family

What is the prime responsibility of the disciple: the family or the church? Such a question might be difficult for many. There are churches that teach and encourage their parishioners to put the church first. After all, didn't Jesus declare, "Who are My mother and brothers? You are My brothers." Didn't Jesus say, "Unless you leave mother and father for Me, you cannot be My disciple"? These are ways texts are manipulated and lead followers astray.

I have witnessed individuals who have found G_d and abandoned their families in His name. Parents had no burial plans; children went without food, while the church collected money from those who neglected their families. "Honor your father and mother." Do not seek to uplift humanity while you neglect those you are first responsible for. Many have given to the church, and when they have asked the church for assistance, none was given.

It may be argued that the church is family and is made up of families. This is true. But I have also seen inequities in the treatment of families. Some families may be more prestigious than others. Some families may have pedigrees and benefit from the church because of their statuses. These are just the realities that go on in the house of G_d.

Usury/Interest

A nefarious practice that takes place in poorer communities is payday loans. People borrow against their paychecks to make a necessary purchase. The loans are often given at a high interest rate. Individuals take out these loans because they are unable to secure a more traditional loan.

Because of a consumer mindset facilitated by a capitalist structure, many live off credit cards that carry 22 percent to 25 percent interest rates. They sink deeper and deeper into debt. They may consolidate their loans into one payment, but because they haven't addressed their habits and the mindsets that governs them, they continue to live on credit cards. But they now owe the credit card companies in addition to the consolidated loans. The church says to return tithes and offerings from your increase. However, they treat income as increase. Income is not increase when you're in debt.

Surety/Cosign

A surety is a person who secures payment for someone else who has taken out a loan. In essence, he is a cosigner. "Do not be one of those who shakes hands in a pledge, one of those who is a surety for debts." Do not cosign a loan for a friend, and be careful if you cosign a loan for a family member. Do not loan money to anyone; you are not a bank. If you choose to help someone financially, let it be based on what you do not need. Do not give and leave yourself in need. Money changes people, and loaned money changes relationships.

Give to those in need; give to a cause. Help elevate humanity, but do not sign your name to any document that lists you as a surety for someone else's debt. If you are in a relationship but not married, do not tie your money together. Do not sign any papers for the person you think you love. Do not share a credit card or give one access to your credit card. And women, if you date a man who needs to borrow money from you when you are dating … run! And men, if you are dating a woman who needs to borrow money from you … run!

These are basic principles that the Word of G_d has given to us to guide us in our responsibilities with money. Our responsibilities do not begin and end with church tithes and offerings, especially when other principles have been neglected.

The Cheerful Giver

"So let each one give as he purposes in his heart, not grudgingly or of necessity; for G_d loves a cheerful giver." This is the governing principle in the mind of the believer. The attitude of the believer is governed by the gratefulness of the sacrifice of Christ, not the obligation to the church.

Unfortunately, a capitalistic mindset has infiltrated the church of the living G_d, and scripture is now used to promote a false teaching. Giving is now based on reciprocity. You hear it from the television evangelists: Sow a seed, and you will get back more. Give a tithe and an offering so that G_d will open the windows of heaven to you. When the reality is none of these, texts are grounded in financial blessings.

"Press down, shaken together, running over" is a text dealing with how people are treated. How you treated people will be meted back to you, pressed down, shaken together, and running over in good measure! Too many have been led astray by teachers whose only purpose is to separate them from their finances. It may be an individual preacher, or it may be a system. Both are evil as they seek to control and manipulate people.

No wonder people are tired and miserable. They give 15 percent to the church and then must pay exorbitant tuition fees for their children to receive a quality education. Then they are asked to give to a building fund that never seems to get done. It grinds on the spirit and attitude of the giver. But there is hope. There is an ability to give to the cause of G_d from a heart of gratitude without being manipulated into how much you must give.

How much could you give to the cause of Christ if you didn't have your debt? How much would you give to the cause of Christ if you were not trying to live beyond your means? Money influences your attitude. You know that when you have money, your disposition is more pleasant. But when you don't have money, you sometimes feel depressed. It's dangerous to allow money to control your attitude.

Look at our society. People must buy; people must spend. People go to malls even when they don't need anything. People look to upgrade devices, clothes, and so on, even when their items are less than a year old. Buying and spending is a spiritual exercise that many do not even realize they are engaging in. This cannot be what governs the spirit of the people of G_d. Our spirits cannot be uplifted by the latest fashions; they cannot be fulfilled by the latest gadgets. We cannot be joyful going to Macy's, Dillard's, Nordstrom's but sad or despondent when giving to the cause of G_d. How many would still give if they did not receive a tax benefit? Let us examine ourselves.

Lessons

- Do not link your money to high-interest loans.
- Your financial responsibility is first to your family.
- Do not cosign for a loan.
- The cheerful attitude of giving should be based on the price that Christ paid to redeem us.

CHAPTER 10

The System of Giving

Do I say these things as a mere man? Or does not the law say the same also? For it is written in the law of Moses, "You shall not muzzle an ox while it treads out the grain." Is it oxen G_d is concerned about? Or does He say it altogether for our sakes? For our sakes, no doubt, this is written, that he who plows should plow in hope, and he who threshes in hope should be partaker of his hope. If we have sown spiritual things for you, is it a great thing if we reap your material things? If others are partakers of this right over you, are we not even more?

—1 Corinthians 9:8–12 NKJV

Every religious organization operates a financial system that pays ministers, teachers, and staff members, as well as offer health-care insurance as regulated by the government system under which they operate. For many of these systems, they use the principle of the tithe to encourage their members to give consistently. This is not necessarily a problem. It is the right of every organization, religious or political, to establish what governs their fiduciary principles. What is not acceptable is teaching something as a biblical principle to mislead the unsuspecting. I do not say this lightly.

We are living in a time of disinformation and misinformation. The two are similar but not the same. Disinformation is false information that is intended to mislead. There is an intent to deceive for the benefit of a person or group promoting the disinformation. We are living in a time of political disinformation. A man has claimed to have won the 2020 US presidential election, even though people in his inner circle told him he lost. Those who know he lost deemed it advantageous to spread the disinformation for the purpose of possibly staying in power.

Those who put their trust in these individuals believe and share the message. Those who support the disinformation believe it and spread it. They do not spread it with the intent of deceiving. They spread it because they believe it. This is misinformation. Misinformation is something that is a lie but believed to be true. Unfortunately, the concepts of disinformation and misinformation are not restricted to the political realm. They also operate in the religious realm.

Bring all the tithe into the storehouse; give of the Lord the firstfruits of your substance; give, and it will be given unto you: good measure, pressed down, shaken together, running over. "Try me now," says the Lord, "if I will not open to you the windows of heaven and pour out a blessing that there will not be room enough to receive it." These are scriptures in the Bible, yet none of them apply to giving to the church.

The apostle Paul affirms the necessity of those who work in the spiritual to be taken care of in the material. Paul declares that the servant is not to be muzzled, that the workman is worthy of his hire. This verifies that religious organizations create models of stewardship based on faithfulness to the Word of G_d, not manipulation of the Word of G_d.

Paul further declares that grievous wolves would come in not sparing the flock. This can also refer to ministers and leaders who are to be served rather than serve. Yes, religion is a dangerous thing. Understanding the scriptures is the duty of each person. Some are reading this right now, and your understanding of what has been written does not reveal the heart of the author. But it does reveal your heart. Do you now believe you don't have to give as much? Do you now believe that the author has undermined the law of G_d? G_d forbid, I establish the law, not as an outside rule to be followed, but one that is found in Christ because He is the end of the law. Christ is our righteousness. Christ is our justification. Christ is our sanctification. You do not keep Christ and the law.

Those who believe this book removes the responsibility of giving always sought an excuse not to give. This book purports that 10 percent does not belong to G_d; 100 percent does. And the giver gives based on what the merits of Christ's life, death, resurrection, and ministry in the heavenly are worth. What is your salvation worth? How is it manifested in how much you spend and what you spend on?

Make a vow unto the Lord and keep that vow. It is better not to make a vow than to make a vow and break it!

Lessons

- Religious organizations have the right to implement a financial structure to maintain their missions. They should not manipulate scripture to take advantage of unsuspecting organizational loyalists.
- Many scriptures that have nothing to do with money are used to encourage monetary giving.
- What you spend your money on at the mall or on Amazon is just as much a statement as returning a tithe.

CHAPTER 11

Weightier Matters

> Woe to you, scribes and Pharisees, hypocrites! For you pay tithe of mint and anise and cumin and have neglected the weightier matters of the law: justice and mercy and faith. These you ought to have done, without leaving the other undone.
>
> —Matthew 23:23 NKJV

A surface reading of Matthew 23:23 would seem to read that Jesus upholds the return of tithe to the local church in the New Testament. However, this is not the case. A clearer picture and understanding will reveal that as Jesus was speaking to the scribes and Pharisees, He had not yet completed the work of the atoning sacrifice. Thus, all the laws that pointed to Him were still to be upheld. Just as He had told the lepers to show themselves to the priest even though they were healed, Jesus upheld the law. The issue of His message was not the returning of tithes but rather, the neglect of weightier matters.

As Jesus declared the various woes to the scribes and Pharisees, He is driving home the point of the danger of religion. One can "do" religion for so long that it no longer represents the change that can take place in a person but instead the playacting that can develop because of being religious.

Engaging in religious life has advantages. It allows one to be respected, and it affords prestige and power. It also amplifies people's trust, which at the same time, makes them vulnerable to predators. People look up to ministers, priests, rabbis, and imams. There is an inherent belief that they are closer to G_d or have greater access to Him. Even though this is not true, it is what many believe.

The ministers of the various faiths have the responsibility to look after the needs of their people and communities. They should understand the needs of the elderly as well as the challenges facing youth and children, all while working with others to uphold justice and mercy. But with so many churches and so many religious leaders, one thing they all have in common is collecting money from their parishioners.

Some have collected money for jets and cars and suits as those who struggle to choose between paying their rent or buying groceries. I know what you are thinking: *Dr. Sylvester, all ministers are not like this.* Maybe not. But the scriptures declare in Revelation 3 that the church is rich and increased with goods and has need of nothing. The church has experienced great monetary benefit, but has it translated into people's lives being improved?

Has the church had anything to say about the rights of minorities being taken away? Has the church addressed the homeless issues in its community? Has the church sought ways to stem gang violence or teenage pregnancy? What has the church had to say about racism, sexism, nepotism, and every other ism? While the church has collected tithes, it has lost the meaning of the tithes and separated itself from justice, righteousness, and mercy. The church does not deal with weightier matters. Why not?

Is it because dealing with weightier matters will force us to confront our family members? Is it because dealing with weightier matters will challenge us to do self-examinations? No longer can we maintain denominational loyalty when that loyalty undermines justice, righteousness, and mercy. Go to a board meeting. Go to a business meeting and weigh what subjects are important enough to be included on the agenda. Is it people trying to keep control of their territories that they have marked out? Have they served in the church so long that they can't stop serving themselves? One member said to me, "Pastor, I'm going to keep on doing what I'm doing until the Lord tells me to stop." Needless to say, the Lord has been trying to get them to stop through many other voices, but they just don't realize it's the Lord's voice.

I love church. Church has been a blessing to me. I had my first kiss in church. I had men to look up to as examples when I had no father in the house. And I have found myself working for the church now for over thirty years. This critique does not come from a place of malice but from a place of love.

People are hurting, and they don't need to sow seeds to prove they are faithful. They don't need to buy handkerchiefs to get blessings. And they don't need to give a mandatory amount as signs of loyalty. They don't need to give of necessity or begrudgingly for G_d loves the cheerful giver. Giving to G_d must be based on the value we put on the sacrifice of the Son of G_d. And in return, the church and its leader must take that sacrificial giving and address weightier matters.

Lessons

- If a church purports to collect tithes but has no message regarding racism, homelessness, financial pilfering of the poor, and so on, that church has never collected tithes.
- The church having money is not a symbol of G_d's blessing. Money has replaced justice even in houses of worship.
- Jesus's words to the priests about returning tithes of mint and anise and cumin were not a command for the church to uphold the practice of giving tithes.

CHAPTER 12

A Message to Seventh-Day Adventists

And every priest stands ministering daily and offering repeatedly the same sacrifices, which can never take away sins. But this Man, after He had offered one sacrifice for sins forever, sat down at the right hand of G_d, from that time waiting until His enemies are made His footstool. For by one offering He perfected those who are being sanctified.

—Hebrews 10:11–14 NKJV

Several ministers have debated with me on this issue. One stated, "Jesus said, regarding the tithe, this you ought to have done without leaving the other undone." This is a reference to Jesus speaking to the Pharisees in Matthew 23, that they pay tithe of mint, anise, and cumin but negate the weightier matter of the law: love, justice, and mercy. He declared, so Christ did not do away with it. He failed to apply the context that this was before He died on the cross. Jesus always upheld the practice of the law, moral and Levitical, prior to the cross.

Some Seventh-day Adventists will read this and believe that the law is being marginalized, and if the tithe is being undermined, the Sabbath will be next. This pattern of thinking reveals that denominational faithfulness is more important than faithfulness to the Word. The scriptures declare, "we can do nothing against the truth, but for the truth." No one can operate a faith-based system out of fear. There are things in scripture that reveal what it means to be *in* Christ, and there are other aspects of scripture that point *to* Christ. Things established by G_d before sin and given to Adam and Eve show what it is to be *in* Christ. The things established after the sin of Adam and Eve primarily point *to* Christ.

I have been enculturated in the Seventh-day Adventist organization. This organization does not use a congregational model of giving. Rather, giving is based on a missional principle. This is important because whatever model a system establishes, it does so to facilitate its mission and vision. It doesn't matter if it is Baptist, Methodist, Pentecostal, or Catholic. The Seventh-day Adventist church came out of the Methodist model system, both financially and structurally. It utilizes the concept of conferences and a general conference.

A congregational model uses the congregation as the primary recipient and allocator of funds collected in the church. The church may be governed by a system that receives a portion of the monies collected. For example, a church may collect $100,000 and give 10 percent, or $10,000, to the organization it belongs to. Congregations may give to the Southern Baptist or General Conference of the Methodist church. However, the responsibility of hiring and paying pastors and covering their expenses falls on the congregation. Not so in the Adventist model.

In the Adventist model, the congregation does not retain any portion of the monies allocated as tithe in the church. Each congregation sends tithe funds to the conference to which it belongs. The conference is made up of a group of churches located in a certain geographical area. It is made up of representatives of the churches, with pastors often elected to serve as presidents and vice presidents. The local church is left to operate its local budget solely on funds allocated as local offerings. In turn, each conference donates 10 percent of the tithes received to what are called unions. Unions are a group of conferences in a certain geographical location. They are primarily tasked with conferring who is ordained ministers in the Seventh-day Adventist church. They also plan and lead growth models for the district in which they operate.

Allow me to use the Seventh-day Adventist model as a premise. It is incumbent on each person to know what system governs the finances they are a part of and have put their faith in. The Adventist system is known to utilize both the Old Testament and New Testament. Adventists see the two testaments as complementing each other. "Here are they that keep the commandments of G_d and have the Testimony of Jesus." This is a description of the remnant, which is how the Adventists see themselves.

The giving system was developed over time. The initial system of Seventh-day Adventists was called "Systematic Benevolence". Initially, the leaders gave 1 percent of the value of their properties and income. As the movement began to grow and obtain more property, they needed to find a way to sustain a more consistent form and system of giving. Early Adventists did not hold to the requirement of the tithe as it would ratify the continuance of the Levitical system. While certain Levitical laws could be traced as existing before man sinned, the tithing system was not one of them.

Ellen White, in her comments on tithes prior to 1876, almost always uses it in the context of systematic benevolence. In 1876, D. M. Canright, one of the leaders, brought a recommendation to the conference:

> Resolved, That we believe it to be the duty of all our brethren and sisters, whether connected with the churches or living alone, under ordinary circumstances, to devote one-tenth of all their income from whatever source, to the cause of G_d. And further

> Resolved, That we call the attention to all our ministers to their duty in this important matter to set it plainly and faithfully before all their brethren and urge them to come up to the requirements of the Lord in this thing.

By the year 1878 a change had been made in the plan of figuring the percentage of giving or tithe, shifting from approximately one percent per year to the total valuation of property to ten percent of the actual income.

It is also worth noting that the early church did not collect money on a Sabbath or on a weekly basis:

> We solemnly promise, before G_d and to each other, conscientiously to pay the Systematic Benevolence treasurer a tithe of all our income, to be laid by when received, and paid on the first Sunday of each one of the four quarters of the year; namely, the first Sunday in January, the first Sunday in April, the first Sunday in July, and the first Sunday in October."

These are just a few examples of the process and the development of financial giving and the premise used to govern the system in the Adventist church. Every denomination has gone through a developmental process using the scripture as the basis for its belief. Today, many Adventists teach that the tithe should only be used for the payment of ministers and teachers. However, consider these words:

> Those churches that have to build houses of worship, and meet the expenses of lights, fuel, etc. and do not feel able to come up to the figures of our illustration of systematic benevolence besides, can at their annual meeting appropriate by vote such a percent of their entire systematic benevolence funds to such objects as they think proper. But it is supposed that the instances where such a course would be necessary would be very few.

The Seventh-day Adventist church was formally organized in 1863. Thirty-eight years later, 1901, the church was restructured to meet the changes of a growing society as it entered the twentieth century. From 1901 to the present, the organizational and financial structures of this religious organization have not changed. Even though the world has changed from an agrarian to an industrial to a digital society, the structures have not changed to facilitate the mission in a changing society.

The church is what the scriptures declares it to be: rich and increased with goods and having need of nothing. It does not realize it is poor, miserable, blind, and naked.

The issue at hand is the support of the gospel. What system should be used? It has been established that the tithes represent righteousness. We have also shown by scripture that the laws governing the priests are not applicable to the ministry of the New Testament. However, the gospel must go forward, and the people of G_d are called to give their all. Thus, this is not a call to no longer give a tithe. Instead, it is a call to the disciple that we have greater responsibilities.

Ten percent does not belong to G_d. One hundred percent belongs to G_d. This is the basis of the New Testament teaching and the value of the cross. The apostle Paul highlights this aspect in his writings, especially in 1 Corinthians 9. He argues that the minister who serves spiritual things has a right to partake in material sustenance. Paul uses an analogy that those who served in the temple had a right to eat of the things of the temple. In the same way, those who preach the gospel should live from the gospel. Paul made this analogy without ratifying the tithes as a crossover obligation in the gospel dispensation. This is because he could not on one hand say that circumcision is nothing, and at the same time, teach the continuance of the tithe.

The principle that guides giving is the value of the death of Christ. Before the cross, giving was based on what Christ would do. The symbols of bread and wine were met with the symbol of the tithe. Because Christ gave His body and blood and removed the shadow of things, we can no longer respond to the body and blood with continual symbols of righteousness. Christ wants payment in full. This is not salvation by works. It is salvation that works. It is the purpose of the giving of His body and blood.

For Seventh-day Adventists, many look at Ellen White to dictate what they should do. And yet, this is a complicated application. Whenever she dealt with tithes, it was in support of the organization's mission and the giver's responsibility to support the gospel. However, she was not a theologian, and she received no visions pertaining to the tithe. In one instance, she declared that givers should not divert their tithes to other causes. But when she saw injustice and unrighteousness being done toward blacks in the South, she redirected her tithes to do justly for that cause. Thus, it may be argued that she understood the true meaning of the tithe in its original context.

Whether Baptist, Methodist, Catholic, or Pentecostal, how is righteousness upheld and facilitated by the monetary practices of the religious organizations? What percentage is dedicated to the poor of its congregation and to the widows, single parents, or foster children? In an age when colonial Christianity creates a deeper divide based on racism, classism, and sexism, now more than ever we need justice and righteousness to roll down like mighty streams. If it cannot be done in houses that declare they know G_d, what hope is there outside those houses?

Lessons

- Give to the cause of G_d.
- Give to that which promotes righteousness and justice.
- Give to the widows, the poor, the orphans, the immigrants, and those who proclaim the gospel.
- Give cheerfully and lovingly.
- Give not to be seen or known but that the lives of others may be improved.

Printed in the United States
by Baker & Taylor Publisher Services